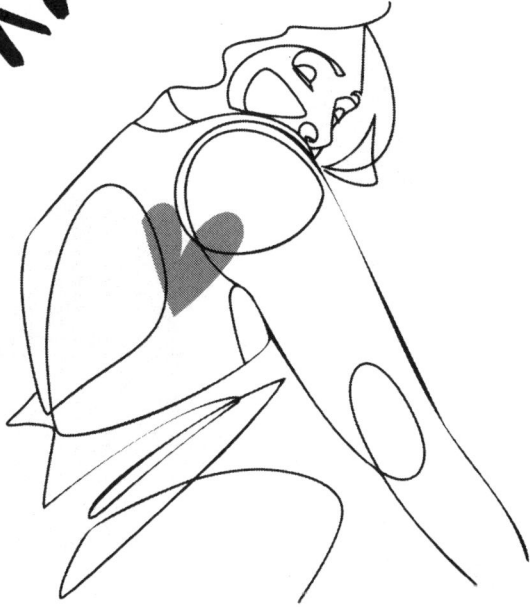

JOURNEY
TO
THE
HEART

TRAUMA HEALING JOURNAL

ANNA MISIEYUK

CONTENT

Journey to the Heart. Trauma Healing Journal
invites you to get in touch with your feelings, reflect deeply and lift your well-being through self-expression and emotional release.
This is a space created with love and care, where your heart can speak and your soul can breathe.

Please note, that this journal is not intended to replace professional support, medical advice or treatment. If you are currently receiving therapy or are under medical care, consult with your therapist or medical professional to ensure that this journal is compatible with your journey to healing.

this journal belongs to:

....

You are here.

not where you used to be,
not yet where you're going,
but here-breathing, feeling, trying.
let this be a place where
you don't have to be strong.
let these pages hold what your heart
has carried for too long.
no rush. no judgment.
just you, meeting yourself where you are.

it's not about going fast,
it's about becoming aware.
it's not about fixing,
because nobody is broken.
it's not about becoming someone new,
but about returning to yourself.
so, give yourself the time you need.
you are not alone in this.
step by step, word by word,
you write your way back to your heart.

and that is more than enough.

The path to healing can be difficult and challenging, but so is carrying the invisible weight that shapes your daily choices and robs you of your sense of agency and freedom. Living from a place of victimhood, unaware of your worth and the power you have to create change, can feel just as heavy. Building intimacy is also difficult when, deep down, are afraid of being hurt again, just as you were before. And it is also painful to live disconnected from yourself-from your emotions, desires, and needs.

We all carry stories that shape us and influence our thoughts, feelings and behavior. Often we don't realize how deeply they are imprinted in our bodies, how their echoes continue to ripple through our everyday lives. The past can be a heavy burden, but it can also become a guide-if we dare to look at it with honesty, without fear and judgment.

This journal was created to give you a space to reconnect with yourself and reclaim your inner strength. Through deep and reflective questions, I invite you to step through a doorway into self-discovery. I believe that questions are like portals-they lead you into different corners of your inner world, helping you uncover who you truly are, what your values are, and what your dreams might be beyond expectations and fears. They inspire, encourage change, and help you seek solutions and take meaningful action. They allow you to get closer to what really matters.

I hope you will find a thought within these pages that resonates with you, that touches something important within you, that helps you see things in a new light. Perhaps one that will lead you back to yourself, to your inner depths, to your heart.

Remember, healing is not a race. It is a gradual process of discovering yourself with tenderness and openness. Allow yourself to pause, to sit with whatever arises-for much may arise. A wide range of emotions will accompany you. Give yourself permission to feel them. They are part of you. Do not fear them-welcome them, listen to them, give them space. Every emotion matters. Each one has something to tell you. Each has its place in your healing journey.

I am grateful that you are here and that you have made the decision to meet yourself. I celebrate your choice to show up for yourself, to step out of hiding, and to go on a date with life. Within the pages of this journal, I invite you to look at yourself without filters and to discover your own truth. You will explore different aspects of your life, emotions, and experiences. This also means facing your past and acknowledging it as a part of your story-embracing it rather than hiding from it or fearing it. I believe that it is in truth, in the rawness of being, that the transition into light begins.

Healing is a conscious inner process-one that is not about fighting yourself but about making peace with who you are. It is about seeing yourself with your heart, not just your mind, and saying:

I see you.
I accept you.
I love you.

And if today you are not able to make peace with what you have been through, if you cannot yet look at your past with gentleness, and if it is still difficult for you to accept what happened - that's okay too. Do not force yourself to close wounds before they are ready, to pretend that something no longer hurts when you can still feel it inside.Maybe today, the only thing you can do is acknowledge that it was hard. Maybe it's enough to simply notice your emotions, even if they are painful, and allow them to exist.

Healing takes time, space, and readiness. Just recognizing that something within you is shifting, that something longs to change, is already a beginning. Your conscious choice-Yes, I want this-is the first step on a journey where you may stumble, but each fall will make you stronger, bringing you closer to yourself, teaching you to love and accept yourself-fully and completely.

the power of the written word

Writing is a form of release. It allows us to let go of negative thoughts and emotions, guiding us toward greater clarity and inner peace.

Putting our beliefs, feelings, and memories on paper-honestly and without filters-is like having an open conversation with a dear friend, or even better - with ourselves. In a way, it's like therapy. I like to call it an inner cleansing ritual, though at times, it feels more like an emotional dumping ground. Writing helps us process what we feel, accept every emotion without denying or diminishing it, and confront our wounds instead of burying them in silence.

Writing about difficult experiences helps us make sense of them and imagine a new path forward. It reduces stress, anxiety, and sadness, improving our overall well-being. Numerous studies have shown that simply putting our struggles into words can bring relief. Naming our emotions and describing them with clarity means bringing them into the light, stripping them of their destructive power.

Journaling is an act of self-care. Expressing yourself through writing means engaging in a dialogue with your soul, diving deep within, and rediscovering yourself. It allows us to explore who we are, recognize unconscious patterns, emotional blocks, or limiting beliefs we may not even be aware of.

In the fast-paced world we live in, it's easy to get lost in the chaos and disconnect from ourselves. That's why developing self-awareness and learning to recognize our thoughts and feelings is so important.

As you embark on this journey of self-reflection, you will turn your gaze inward, focusing on what truly matters: **YOURSELF**. Your needs, dreams, and strengths. I want to guide you into a space of authenticity and care.

9

The answers you seek won't always come immediately. Sometimes, they will require deep introspection. You don't have to figure everything out at once. But if you choose to be honest with yourself, you will find your way. You certainly don't have to answer every question right away. Give yourself as much time as you need. Don't rush. There may be moments when you're not ready to explore certain places in your heart or mind. So don't force yourself to dive in if it feels too difficult.

Be patient, gentle and understanding with yourself. Allow yourself to capture meaningful thoughts and pour them onto paper. Return to them the next day and see what new insights they bring. How both the questions and your own answers continue to work within you.

If I may share my experience in finding myself, journaling has been deeply therapeutic for me. Writing has transformed my life, and it continues to do so. When I put my thoughts and emotions into words, I feel lighter, as if something inside me has been set free. Writing has saved me more than once, helping me find a new direction. It has taught me to experience my emotions in a healthy way-not to suppress them, but to move through them with awareness.

It walks with me through difficult moments, creating space for calm, allowing me to let go, and helping me care for wounds that are still healing. It is not a magical cure, but it is part of an ongoing journey-one in which I continue to rebuild myself, piece by piece.

Thank you for allowing me to walk this path with you toward greater self-awareness. With all my heart, I hope it leads you toward a lighter, more balanced life.

But remember–
You are your own best guide.

Listen to your heart—it always knows the way.

Journey to the Heart: Trauma Healing Journal is designed

- for those who carry wounds from the past, seeking a path to healing, relief from emotional pain, and a renewed sense of peace.

- for those who want to free themselves from the past and let go of what no longer serves them, taking a step toward a new beginning with compassion and courage.

- for those who long to truly feel their emotions–to recognize, understand, and accept them without fear, creating a deeper connection with themselves and others.

- for those overwhelmed by racing thoughts, daily worries, and uncertainty about the future–yearning to find inner peace and stillness.

- for those who have lost touch with their true essence, trapped in the expectations of others, and now feel the need to rediscover their authenticity and truth.

- for those who wish to know themselves on a deeper level, develop greater self-awareness, align with their inner wisdom, and reconnect with who they are at their core.

- for those who want to learn to love and accept themselves unconditionally, recognize their worth and inner beauty, and build a relationship with themselves rooted in kindness and strength.

- **for her, for him, for you.** To start writing, to give space to your feelings, your dreams, and your reflections–without judgment, without fear.

Create a Safe and Loving Space

Find a quiet, comfortable place where you feel at ease and won't be disturbed. If you'd like, light a candle or your favorite incense to create a peaceful atmosphere. Soft background music may help you relax. Prepare your favorite infusion or coffee-whatever brings you comfort.
This is your intimate moment-a space where you can explore yourself and reconnect with your inner world, feeling completely safe. Allow yourself to settle into this space fully. Take a deep breath. Let go of expectations. Simply be present with whatever arises.

Be Honest with Yourself

Let your thoughts and emotions flow freely, without judgment. When you write, be open and sincere-allow yourself to express what you truly feel. Remember, this is for you and you alone. You don't have to prove anything to anyone, nor do you need to justify yourself.
Give yourself time to find the answers. Some insights may come instantly, while others might take longer to surface. Accept every impression, emotion, and inner reaction that arises. Trust the process. Write them down, even if they seem unclear at first. Each word you put on paper is a step toward deeper understanding.

If it helps, you can tear the page and throw it away. Sometimes, destroying what we've written can help release the emotional weight we carry inside. It can be a symbol of a new beginning-letting go of what no longer serves you, bringing a sense of relief.
Every thought and emotion has the right to exist. Don't judge them-just let them be. Whatever you feel is valid. If tears come, let them flow; crying is a way to cleanse and free yourself. Be gentle and patient with yourself, and embrace your authenticity.

Don't Worry About Grammar

Just write. Put your pen to paper and let the words pour out. Don't worry about grammar or spelling-that's not what matters. Don't stop to correct mistakes or wonder if what you're writing makes sense. Simply allow your thoughts and feelings to pour onto the page.

Seek Professional Support if Needed

If writing about certain topics feels particularly difficult or emotionally overwhelming, and you feel like you can't handle it alone, consider reaching out to a therapist or counselor. Asking for help is an act of courage and self-love.

let your pen be guided by emotion,
and not by perfection.

WHAT IS MY WHY?

Set a clear intention before you begin, as it will serve as a guiding light and grounding force that will bring you back to your core focus whenever you feel overwhelmed by your thoughts, emotions, or experiences.

I hope...

when the weight of the world
presses down on your chest,
when pain slips into places
you've hidden even from yourself,
that you choose - not what they want,
but what you need.
I hope you find the courage
to step out from the crowd,
and build a path from your true,
though broken parts
that leads back to your own heart.

Close your eyes, listen to what your heart is telling you,
and ask yourself:

WHAT DO I TRULY FEEL INSIDE?

How do I deal with it?

HOW WOULD I LIKE TO FEEL?

what can I do for myself to feel this way?
How can I give myself a helping hand?

to do:

Find a moment of joy in your day, no matter how fleeting it may be.

HOW DOES LIFE TREAT ME?   HOW DO I TREAT MY LIFE?

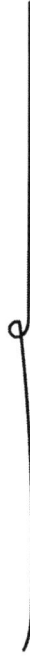

what within me is ripening
and ready to come into the light?

Do I really know myself?

i know many things,
but i know little,
or maybe nothing at all,
about myself.
i am a puzzle to be solved,
i take one step forward a day,
and often one step back.

you are a miracle,
you are not a small thing.
you are the most beautiful miracle.
you are the expression of God.
you need do nothing but be,
you are all that is needed.

it is not your body,
it is not your name,
it is not your title
that enchants us.
look at the rainbow after the rain.
who doesn't stop to admire it?
it exists, and that is enough.

WHO AM I?

I AM . . .

I FEEL . . .

I DO . . .

I LOVE . . .

I NEED . . .

I WANT . . .

I CAN . . .

I UNDERSTAND . . .

I SPEAK . . .

I SEE . . .

I KNOW . . .

I ALLOW . . .

the lie i live in

isn't spoken–
it's in my choices
that aren't mine.
it's in the "yes"
when i mean "no,"
in the boundaries
i fail to set,
in suppressed needs
and passions
whose wings i cut.
it hides behind
forced smiles,
seeking approval,
pretending to be
someone i'm not.
the lie is the mask
i wear to be liked,
the part of me
that stays silent
when i'm aching to speak.

it's the life i live for others,
–not for myself.

THE LIES I HIDE BEHIND?

WHAT IS MY TRUTH?

your truth may be imperfect,
but it is yours
- rooted in who you are,
not who you should be.

Close your eyes and turn inward. Can you recall a moment when you felt completely in tune with yourself, when you simply knew who you were and what you wanted? A moment when clarity replaced doubt, and your heart felt wide open. Let this memory rise to the surface and try to write about it.

the truth doesn't scream, it whispers to you.

what story do I tell myself about myself?

---

the story you tell
is it a story about being strong,
carrying more than you should,
never asking for help?
or is it about searching,
belonging everywhere and nowhere,
being never enough?
what if your story could change?
where strength meets care,
struggle turns into being at peace,
& gratitude is greater than resilience.

the story you tell matters.

make sure it serves you.

I TRULY FEEL MYSELF WHEN. . .

let yourself be free!

freedom is being yourself,
your truest, unconditional self.
your heart was not made
to be in a cage.
stop shrinking yourself
and raise your voice.
take your space.
and if the world wants you
to be different,
be even more yourself.

you were born to live, not to hide.

DO I FULLY ACCEPT MYSELF?

whatever flower you are,
when your time comes, you will bloom.
accept as you are at this moment,
our imperfections become our beauty.

when you cut off parts of yourself,
trying to fit into the shape
of someone else's idea of
enough,
necessary,
appropriate,
worthy,
attractive,
excellent,
strong,
successful
...
-pause.

go back to your heart
and look from its perspective.

you are already complete.
complete in your own becoming.

If there were no such thing as judgment,
would I see myself differently?

what stops me from embracing myself completely?

try to
see your worth
beyond the layers of doubt,
to stand in the sunlight,
proud of every scar,
to embrace the imperfections,
letting the light fall on them.
try to
sit with the pieces
you once wanted to hide
and say:

"you're welcome here."

because
you were never meant to be perfect,
but real.

WHAT PARTS OF ME HAVE I HIDDEN TO FIT IN,
and how can I bring them back into the light?

everything you seek outside of you already exists within.
look inward and feel it.

Imagine a life where you feel completely free to be yourself-without fear, without expectations, without the need to fit into any mold. Who would you be if nothing held you back? How would you move through the world? What parts of yourself would shine the brightest?

IF I COULD BE MY TRUE SELF, WHO WOULD I BE THEN?

Take a moment to connect with yourself and write down affirmations that will teach you to talk to yourself in a way that strengthens your inner voice. Fill the page with sentences that empower you, affirm your worth, honor your true self, and support you in living authentically.

It all starts with how you feel about yourself.

Strange, isn't it? We know how to love others so easily, but when it comes to ourselves, it becomes incredibly difficult. We give our time, attention, and energy to those around us, often forgetting the most important relationship of all: the one we have with ourselves. Yet, from the first to the last breath, you are the only person you'll spend every single moment of your life with. From start to finish, the only bond that is 100% guaranteed is the one you share with yourself.

How you treat yourself and how you feel about yourself changes everything. When you start to truly love yourself, your energy shifts, your light expands, and the right people can feel it. You attract those who know how to respect you and appreciate you for who you truly are. When you put yourself first and stop settling for unbalanced relationships or people who don't value you, you begin to draw closer to those who are aligned with your worth. And most importantly, you start to understand that the respect and love you seek outside of yourself begin within.

But loving yourself doesn't mean being perfect. It doesn't mean constantly chasing the "best version of yourself." Loving yourself means accepting yourself as you are, with all of your shades, with the light and the shadows that live within you. It means choosing yourself every day, looking at yourself with kindness, and recognizing your greatest value: the simple, extraordinary fact of just being alive.

love,
the one that stays,
begins here-
in the silence of awareness
that you are the loving
and loved.

love begins
with you for you,
with the words:
I see you.

WHAT IS THE MOST HONEST THING I FEEL ABOUT MYSELF?

*Allow yourself to be gentle with yourself
as you would with someone you love.*

WHAT DOES IT MEAN FOR ME TO LOVE MYSELF?

"To love oneself is the beginning of a lifelong romance."

-Oscar Wild

HOW MUCH DO I LOVE MYSELF?
how can I show myself more love?

_____

_____

_____

_____

_____

_____

_____

_____

HOW CAN I BETTER SUPPORT MYSELF
in the difficulties I am currently facing?

liking yourself is a feeling.
but loving yourself is something you do.

How do I take care of myself on a daily basis?

what changes can I make to take better care
of my physical and mental health?

Imagine what it would be like if you spent more time listening to yourself instead of speaking. As if you were your own best friend, who is always ready to understand and support you. Think about how it would feel to know that your emotions are acknowledged, not dismissed; that your thoughts and feelings matter, rather than being criticized; that your experiences hold meaning. Imagine that instead of scolding yourself for mistakes, you could understand and forgive yourself. Isn't it wonderful to know that you can rely on yourself and be your own source of support?

WHAT IS MY BODY ASKING FOR?

what does my heart need?

WHAT IS MY MIND SEEKING?

Loving words that my self longs to hear from me

- I see you, I hear you, I honor you

- you're okay, I like you

- you don't need to prove your worth to anyone

- your value is inherent

- I trust you, and I am proud of how far I've come

- I will be patient with you, we are in this together

- one step at a time is enough

- I believe in you, even when you don't

- your story matters

- you are doing the best you can

- you are worthy of the love you give and receive

- you deserve to rest, heal, and nurture yourself

- don't rush, breath

- I am always by your side

-

-

-

-

-

-

-

-

How do you feel about these words:
"I AM WORTHY OF LOVE"?

You can search the entire universe and not find a single being more worthy of love than you.

-Buddha

Gift yourself a moment of pure love and care by writing a heartfelt letter to your soul.
Honor the divine essence within you with kind and grateful words, recognizing that you are a unique and precious being.

love yourself first and all that you need will follow.

THE HUG I NEED?

now give yourself that hug.

take a big, deep breath, open your arms wide and wrap them around your body from side to side as tightly as you like. feel it like the hug you need.

IF I HAD TO DESCRIBE MYSELF TO SOMEONE WHO DOESN'T KNOW ME,

what 5 words would I use to describe myself?
what represents me the most?

Why did I choose them?

What are the strengths, talents, or unique traits that make you, you? Write down the best things about yourself–big or small, seen or unseen. Let yourself acknowledge and celebrate them fully.

CAN I ALLOW MYSELF TO BE IMPERFECT AND STILL SEE MY OWN WORTH?

Write about the ways in which your imperfections make you unique, human, and beautiful.

you don't have to be perfect to be worthy. your value is not something you can lose or gain. you cannot increase or decrease it, you can only forget about it. you are a unique expression of life, unlike anyone else, and that is your gift. every part of you - your strengths, your struggles, your imperfections - makes you whole. embrace them. you are worthy just as you are.

love yourself in your wholeness.

Consider how you define your own worth, beyond achievements or external validation. What emotions come up when you say "I am enough"? Do you feel resistance, or do you feel a sense of peace? Reflect on any moments where you've doubted your value or felt inadequate. Why do you think those feelings arose?

what does the phrase "I am enough" truly mean to me,

I AM ENOUGH!

Allow yourself to sit with this thought. How does your body respond when you embrace this truth? What changes occur in your mindset when you accept that you are enough, just as you are? How does it feel to fully accept your worth without the need to prove anything? What does it feel like to embrace yourself completely, to say "I am enough" and truly believe it? Sink into this feeling.

What images arise when you think of yourself as whole and complete? Can you capture this feeling in words or through a drawing? Let your imagination guide you to a place where you are unapologetically yourself.

Instead of a to-do list, today I create a to-be list.

I WANT TO BE:

- *happy,*
- *healthy,*
- *kind,*
- *authentic,*
- *compassionate,*
- *grateful,*
- *peaceful,*
- *resilient,*
- *present,*
-
-
-
-
-
-
-
-
-
-
- ***MYSELF.***

WHAT WORDS FLOWING FROM MY HEART DO I NEED TO HEAR TODAY?

pause for a moment and feel your heartbeat—
it always speaks from a place of love and truth.

Emotions are essential part of our journey through life. If we learn to listen to them, they will show us the way and make the path we walk a little lighter. Each emotion has a purpose and carries important information that can help us understand ourselves better. Pain, for example, can teach us where our boundaries lie and reveal the parts of ourselves that need healing, care, and attention. Sadness, on the other hand, shows us what matters to us, while love gives us a sense of meaning and belonging. Anger can reveal unmet needs and parts of ourselves that have not been fully perceived or recognized.

Rather than pushing emotions away, try to listen to them. When you listen to your feelings, you are essentially listening to yourself. Sometimes it is a dialogue about your values and needs; other times it may be about threats. Your emotions are not random; they arise for a reason. The better you recognize and understand these connections, the better you will be able to manage your reactions and make conscious decisions.

In the healing process, it is important not only to understand and accept your emotions but also to allow yourself to feel them. Unexpressed emotions never die. If they are repressed, they are buried alive and later surface in a more harmful way. Suppressing or ignoring pain does not make it disappear; instead, it transforms into a force that shapes your life, often leading to even more suffering.

So allow yourself to feel and accept your emotions, even the difficult ones. Allow yourself to cry, to be angry, to be sad, to be frustrated. These feelings are part of your journey. Remember that it is in fully experiencing them that you will find the peace and understanding you need for true emotional freedom.

emotions are not to be fought.

sit with them, feel their depth,
let them move as they need to.
allow them to be.

in surrender, you release.
in letting go, you find relief.

Write about a particularly intense emotion you've experienced recently. Don't tell the story of what triggered it, but immerse yourself in the heart of the emotion itself. How did it manifest in your body? Did you feel tension in any specific area? Maybe a knot in your throat, a weight on your chest, or trembling hands? How did your heart react? How did your senses perceive what was around you? And what thoughts came to your mind? What words, images, or memories took form? Don't judge what you felt. Embrace it with kindness and give it a voice.

Choose words that reflect or are related to your most common emotions and feelings.

Happy   surprised   fearful

accepted   disgusted   sad

Angry   bored   scared

stressed   critical   Optimistic

disapproving

playful   excited   proud   hurt

Anxious   insecure   frustrated

bitter   tired

isolated   rushed

embarrassed   loving   energetic

worthless   curious   fragile   overwhelmed

grief

joyful   inspired   inferior   let down   guilty

disappointed   vulnerable

Successful   thankful   furious

frightened   Excluded

jealous   peaceful

eager   amazed   confused

violated

confident   hopeful   valued

abandoned   sceptical

Courageous   pressured

exposed   worried   nervous

provoked   lonely

weak   Yearning   Submission

Interested   respected   loved

judgmental   creative

satisfied   astonished   persecuted   free

56

What emotions do you experience dominate, do they strengthen you, nourish you, fulfill you, or exhaust you? Think about their roots, where do they come from?

feelings come and go, like passing visitors.

The hardest emotions for me are...

HOW DO I USUALLY RESPOND TO THEM?

do I allow myself to feel them, or do I try to push them away?
what patterns or coping mechanisms do I notice in myself?

i know they can cause pain,
but meet them,
embrace them,
take care of them.
emotions are guides.
if you learn to listen to them,
they will show you the way.

IS THERE SOMETHING I NEED TO ALLOW MYSELF TO FEEL?

what are the ways I tend to escape from my emotions?

WHAT AM I AFRAID WILL HAPPEN IF I FULLY FEEL THIS EMOTION?

FEEL YOUR EMOTIONS IN THE BODY.

If you had to pinpoint them, where do you feel them most? Do you feel sadness more in your eyes or your heart? And anger in your stomach or throat? What place does shame occupy? And how does your body perceive joy? Choose a color for each emotion.

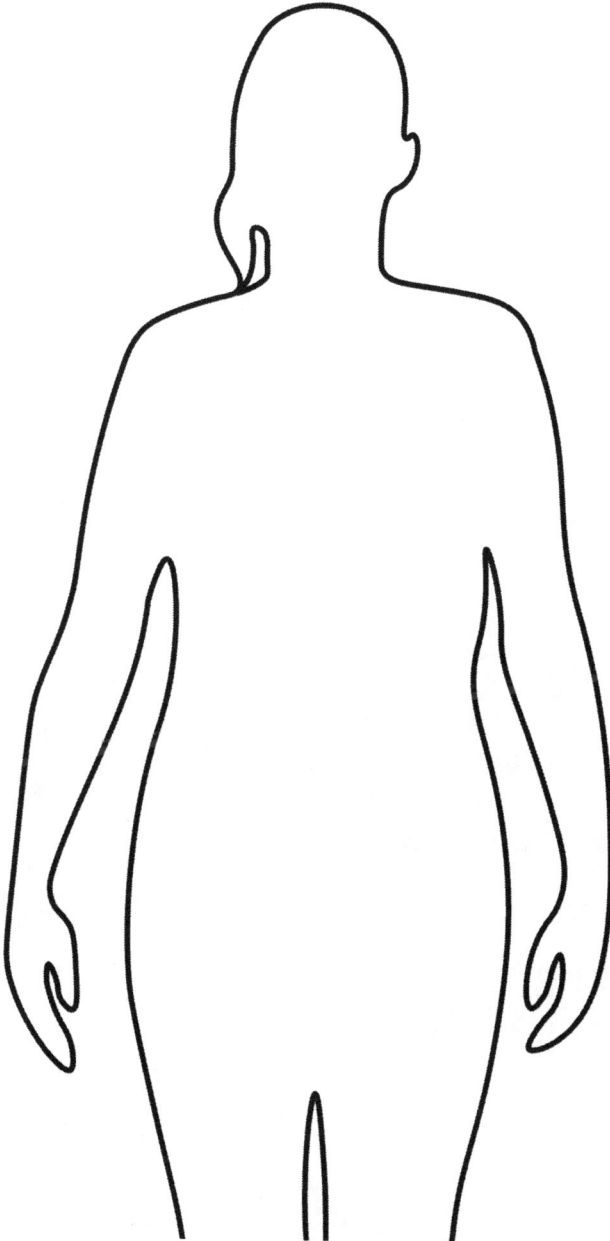

QUICK EMOTIONAL CHECK-IN WITH YOUR BODY

- **Pause and notice** - Take a moment whenever you feel the need to get in touch with your body. Do you feel any tension, tightness, or heaviness anywhere? Where do you sense it the most?

- **Name what you feel** - Try to connect the physical sensation to an emotion. What might have triggered it?

- **Breathe consciously** - Slow, deep breathing can help release tension and bring you back into your body. Notice how your breath moves through you.

- **Express through movement** - Sometimes emotions need movement to be processed. Stretch, dance, shake off stress, or go for a walk to reconnect with yourself.

- **Ask your body** - If you feel tension in a certain area, gently ask yourself, "What are you trying to tell me?" and see what thoughts or feelings arise.

Your body knows - long before you're fully aware of it.
It feels your emotions and holds onto them in ways you may not even realize. Whether it's tightness in your chest when you're anxious or a heaviness in your stomach when you're stressed, your body always shows you what's going on inside. Pay attention to these signals, as they are the first whispers of your emotions. Try to return to your body when you feel an emotion taking over. It will help you recognize and understand it better.

Think about the role emotions play in your life. What do they teach you about yourself? How do they guide you through difficult moments? How do they influence the decisions you make and the relationships you choose? What would it be like if you fully honored them? Then finish the sentence

My emotions are important to me because...

layer by layer,
with the brush of the soul,
I paint my truth.
on the canvas of the heart
I show the image
of my inner world.

Paint the heart and what surrounds it with various emotions that resonate with you. Instead of words, use colors and shades that truly express your feelings. They are your colors, your emotions, the language of your authentic being.

When was the last time I felt joy?
what brought about this moment of joy?

What emotions did I experience alongside joy?
Sometimes joy is accompanied by other feelings.
Did you feel relief, excitement, or even gratitude at the time?

WHAT BRINGS JOY TO MY HEART?
how can I create more of it in my life?

What kind of people or communities make you feel uplifted and energized? How can you spend more time with them or foster these connections in your life?

How do I express joy?

Do I allow myself to feel it fully?

enjoy the little things in life.
one day,
you will see
that they weren't little at all.

WHEN WAS THE LAST TIME I CRIED?

What emotions were involved?

Tears are a natural way for our body and mind to release built-up inner tension. They're not a sign of weakness, but rather proof that we're sensitive and capable of feeling deeply. Crying helps cleanse us, allowing us to let go of what we've held inside for too long, restoring emotional balance and bringing back inner harmony.

when do I allow myself to cry?

dear, let yourself cry.
it is your soul's way of letting go,
it's your heart's way of speaking
when words fall short.

let your tears flow.
let them trace your cheeks,
let them reach the very core.
let them cleanse your wounds,
let them water the hope.

WHERE IS MY SADNESS COMING FROM?
is there anything in particular that triggers it?

What message comes from my sadness?

Sometimes the weight of sadness can feel overwhelming and hard to bear. If you need it right now, allow your sadness to express itself on paper in any form. You can write, draw, or sketch what you're feeling. Whatever helps you release it. There's no wrong way-just allow yourself to do it and give yourself the space to feel.

HOW DO I FEEL SADNESS IN MY BODY?

WHAT THOUGHTS ARISE WHEN I AM SAD?

Sadness is your mind and body's way of telling you that something matters to you. It shows you where your soul has been touched.

sadness needs to be felt.

don't push it away,
don't run from it.
let it flow through you.
suppressing it
can extend the pain.
feel its soar,
feel its fall.
until quiet will return.

emotions are like waves
-they rise, peak, and recede.

DO I ALLOW MYSELF TO FEEL SADNESS FULLY,

or do I try to avoid it?

when I'm feeling low, my heart craves...

_____
_____
_____
_____
_____
_____
_____
_____
_____
_____

WHAT BRINGS ME RELIEF AND SUPPORT
when I am feeling sad?

WHEN SADNESS KNOCKS:

Accept it, without judgment. It's okay to feel this way.

Feel it and observe it. Be with it, breathe through it, and listen to what it has to tell you.

Give yourself time. Don't rush to "get over it." Give yourself space to be in this feeling. Don't fight it; surrender to it. Let it pass on its own.

Take care of yourself. Don't punish yourself or seek casual distractions. Instead, nurture yourself through rest, engaging in your passions, having meaningful conversations, or spending time in nature.

Ask for support. You don't have to be alone with this. There is nothing wrong with reaching out for help.

P.s.
I hope it helps you, as it helps me.

IS THERE ANOTHER EMOTION BEHIND MY SADNESS?
(mayby I also feel anger, shame, or guilt?)

WHAT AM I TRULY ANGRY ABOUT?

WHAT MY ANGER IS TRYING TO TELL ME?

What underlying hurt or fear might be fueling this emotion?
What boundary might have been crossed that triggered your anger?

there is an anger
which has nothing to do
with malice.
it is the roar of someone
*who is defending
his own fragility.*

-Oriana Fallaci

How do I typically respond when I feel angry?
Do I express it openly, or do I tend to hold it in?

How does anger affect my life and relationships?

List at least five situations or triggers that consistently fuel your anger? Then, list at least five healthy actions, thoughts, or habits that help you feel calmer or more in control when anger arises.

Write a message to the person or situation that really makes you mad. Let it all out, no filters, no holding back. This isn't for anyone else, just for you to release all that frustration. Once you've put it down, take a deep breath and let yourself process those feelings without judgment.

Just keep on drawing the line. If you'd like, you can close your eyes. Keep going, and just let your emotions flow.

IN WHAT WAYS DO I EXHAUST MYSELF AND RUN MYSELF
into the ground?

what drives me to it?

everything feels like too much,
& yet nothing is ever enough.
i'm stuck in my head,
exhausted, and so hopeless.
the days blur together,
each one heavier than the last.
caught in this toxic chase,
i've burned myself out.

now, with an empty chest—
no heart to feel,
no lungs to catch a breath,
i miss all of myself.

—but maybe, just maybe,
I'm not lost—just on my way home.

Sometimes, when life feels tough, demanding, and noisy, we long for a quiet haven - even if it exists only in our mind or heart - where we can feel held, grounded, and gently reminded that we are safe. A space where nothing needs to be explained. Where we can soften, breathe, and simply be.

Take a moment to reflect on your emotional refuge - a place, feeling, memory, or presence that brings you comfort when the world feels overwhelming.

What makes me feel safe?

DO I MAKE MY NEEDS A PRIORITY?
what needs do I keep putting off for later (or never)?

List 10 self-care ideas that you can implement to help
yourself get out of or prevent being overwhelmed.

hey, you, i'm here!
you can't keep ignoring me like this.
i need your care, your attention,
and your nurturing.
i know you're busy,
but I'm also on your to-do list
-don't forget that.
you can't do this without me.
so, please get in touch with me.

-your emotional side.

A RISK I NEVER DARED TO TAKE?

in my doubting heart
i hear a voice saying:
"you really could be happy".

i could,
but I'm afraid.

WHAT AM I AFRAID OF?

ARE THESE FEARS BASED ON A REAL THREAT

or driven by my imagination or past experiences?

WHAT IS THE WORST-CASE SCENARIO?

And what if? So what?

when was the last time I felt fear?
what happened, and what triggered it?

WHAT OTHER EMOTIONS ACCOMPANIED IT?

HOW DO I FEEL PHYSICALLY AND EMOTIONALLY WHEN I AM ANXIOUS?

can I observe and accept it with curiosity and without judgment?

How does fear show up in my daily life?

what areas does it affect (e.g., relationships, career, personal growth)?

WHAT DEEPER BELIEF OR THOUGHT MIGHT BE AT THE ROOT OF MY FEAR
(e.g., fear of failure, rejection, uncertainty)?

WHAT HELPS ME FEEL SAFE, STEADY, OR COMFORTED WHEN FEAR, ANXIETY, or uncertainty show up in my life?

When I feel afraid, I need...

SIMPLE STEPS TO CALM YOUR MIND AND BODY
in the face of fear

Focus on your breathing

Take a few slow, deep breaths to calm your mind and body.
Breathe in deeply through your nose, hold it for a moment, and
then breathe out slowly through your mouth. Concentrate on
the rhythm of your breathing. You can try the 4-7-8 technique:
Inhale for 4 seconds, hold for 7 seconds, and exhale for 8
seconds. Repeat a few times.

Ground yourself in the present moment

Scan your body for tension. Start at your toes and move up to
your head, gently releasing any areas of tension. Concentrate
on what you feel physically - this can help you break away
from overwhelming thoughts and restore balance.

Another grounding technique is to connect with your
surroundings. Take note of the things, colors, sounds, and
smells around you. Fully engage your senses - this can bring
your attention to the here and now.

Talk about it

Find a trusted person with whom you can share your feelings.
If you can't speak to anyone, try journaling. Expressing your
emotions allows them to flow and can help you gain clarity.
Sometimes just putting your thoughts into words can make
things feel less heavy.

what could help me face my fear and overcome it?
who or what could make it feel a little easier?

feel the fear, but
don't let it stop you.
it is there to test you,
not to break you.
just because you are afraid
doesn't mean
you are not capable.

think about it.
one brave breath at a time.

Can I find the courage to step to the other side of the fear
that is blocking me and let it guide me?

IF I COULD CONQUER MY FEAR AND ANXIETY,
what would I dare to do?

the moment you replace
fear with curiosity
about the unknown
and trust in life,
God, the Universe,
and yourself
is the same moment
you find your true path
-an authentic path
shaped not by others,
but by your own steps

-the path
you were born to walk.

Fill in the blanks with personal affirmations that resonate with you!

WHEN I FEEL AFRAID, I REMIND MYSELF THAT I AM _____

AND _____ I TRUST IN _____

AND I FACE _____.

WHEN I'M SCARED OF _____ I REMIND MYSELF THAT I AM _____

_____, AND _____

AND I HAVE THE STRENGTH TO OVERCOME ANY OBSTACLE.

WHEN I FEAR _____, I REMEMBER THAT _____

AND _____, SUPPORTED BY _____,

AND I DEAL WITH THIS CHALLENGE THANKS TO _____.

WHEN I'M AFRAID OF _____, I RECOGNIZE THAT _____,

AND I AM _____. I FIND STRENGTH IN _____

AND GAIN COURAGE TO _____.

WHEN I FEAR _____, I REMEMBER THAT I AM _____,

AND _____. I RECEIVE SUPPORT FROM _____

AND FOCUS ON _____ TO CONQUER MY FEAR.

WHEN IN THE PAST HAVE I SHOWN COURAGE I DIDN'T KNOW I HAD?

what did I learn about myself from that experience?

sometimes **courage**
is the decision
to step out
of your comfort zone
into the new and unknown,
into the vision
you have of yourself.

& sometimes courage
is the decision
to *give yourself that chance.*

WHAT SMALL STEP COULD I TAKE TODAY TO FACE SOMETHING
I usually avoid?

Is there someone I admire for their courage?
What can I learn from them?

Today, I want to remind myself that I am capable of...

you've carried this for too long,
this burden is not even yours.
they handed it to you
to keep you small.
they wrapped it in:
you should be ashamed,
what will people think?
shh... keep it to yourself.
good girls don't do that,
and boys don't cry.

so you thought it belonged to you.
you believed it was you.

and now? you can put it away.
grow beyond it.
don't let shame rule you.
start breathing freely,
live without apology.

it's time for you to know–
there's nothing wrong with you.

You have always been enough.
even when they told you otherwise.

Shame can be a heavy and painful emotion that often makes us feel small, unworthy, or like we don't belong. It can come after mistakes, misunderstandings, or moments when we felt vulnerable or weak. Sometimes it comes from situations that weren't even our fault, yet we carry it around believing it defines our worth.

When you experience shame related to past events, it's important to approach it with gentleness and compassion toward yourself. Remember, shame does not define you–it's simply an emotion you are experiencing. You are not your past. You are not your mistakes, misunderstandings, or the hurt you may have gone through. Although these experiences, no matter how difficult, are a part of your story, they do not dictate your value. Allow yourself to be kind to yourself and remember that you deserve respect and love, regardless of what has happened in the past.

WHAT SHAME DO I CARRY IN MY BODY AND HEART?

what is the most common trigger of this emotion in my life?

shame is a shadow,
but you are not the darkness.
don't let your past define you.
you are not your injuries.
you are not your struggles.
you are the one who survived.

Please think about where this shame comes from. Is it related to childhood experiences, to your upbringing, or to some difficult events in your life? Is this shame something that has been imposed on you by others (family, society, culture), or is it the result of your own beliefs?

what values that are important to me
might be connected to my shame?

---

what needs or desires might be underlying it?

HOW DID THIS SHAME AFFECT THE WAY I SEE MYSELF?

give yourself a gift...

permission to embrace
that forgotten or hidden
part of you
that's been waiting for you
to take care of it.

If a close friend felt the same way you do, what comforting
words would you share with them?

WHERE DO I FEEL SHAME IN MY BODY?
What physical sensations arise within me?

what thoughts come to mind when I feel it?

WHAT SITUATIONS OR PEOPLE SEEM TO MAKE THIS EMOTION
stronger?

what can help me navigate through the shame
and allow myself to heal and grow from it?

don't lose your life
to a shame
that doesn't serve you.
allow yourself to forgive:
mistakes,
limitations,
beliefs
that you or others
have placed on you.
you are more
than your past,
you are more
than the judgments
that you carry.

you are wonderful
exactly as you are.

always, in every way.

WHAT WOULD HAPPEN IF I LET IT GO?

what are the words i've been waiting to hear all my life?

whatever the words you've been waiting for ...
whisper them to yourself.

i don't think it's about denying
the experiences that shaped you
and rebuilding yourself from scratch.
no, that's not it.
i think it's about seeing
your strength
on days when you felt fragile,
your courage
even when your voice quivered,
your determination
every time you rose again,
your empathy
when you felt completely lost,
your wisdom
in letting go, even through pain,
your resilience
to keep moving forward.

so please, stop telling yourself
you're not enough.
you just underestimate yourself.

you have really done a lot.
you have so much to be proud of.

you will never hear another voice more than your own.... that voice matters. make it a friend that lifts you up, not an enemy that drags you down. what you whisper to yourself has incredible power and influence, so start telling a good story about yourself.

lesson to learn:

our strength and agency arise from a better narrative.

WHAT IS THE TONE OF THE VOICE IN MY HEAD?

note to self:

baby, i'm proud of you

Have you ever asked yourself- what my inner critic is like (that persistent voice whispering doubts, judgments, and fears)? Is it a monster that casts a shadow over your self-confidence? Or is it a fragile, neglected child who lacks love and understanding? This creature has learned to be loud because it thought it would keep you safe that way.

Take a moment and visualize your inner critic, then describe or draw it.

Can you see that it doesn't want to hurt you, but is afraid?

HOW DOES MY INNER CRITIC SHOW UP?

what does my inner critic focus on or point out when it appears?

Your inner critic may always be there, but it's just
a reminder of where you've been, not where you're going.

Does my inner critic make me doubt my abilities or efforts?
If so, how does it do that and why?

first,
recognize your inner critic.

second,
whenever it starts complaining about you,
remind yourself:

I am not my thoughts,
they do not define me.
they are not reality,
they are just thoughts.

third,
you can change them.

WHY SHOULD I START SEEING MY INNER CRITIC

as just another part of me that needs love and care, instead of someone I need to fight against?

in case you've forgotten:

you've come this far.
you did the best you could with what you had.
what you know now, you didn't know then.
if you fall, get back up and try again.
don't settle for less.
whatever goes wrong, don't lose hope.
whatever happens, don't lose love for life.

You are magic all along.

Think back to a time when you succeeded. How did you feel? How did your body feel? What emotions did you feel - pride, relief, joy? Describe this feeling of recognizing your own strength and abilities.

WHAT'S ONE CHALLENGE I'VE FACED THAT PROVES
I'm stronger than I think?

Please, write a letter to your inner critic, offering compassion and understanding. Although it is a part of you, born of pain, it is no longer needed to guide your life. It needs to know that you are enough as you are now and that you can go through life without its protection.

all these doubts were once love...
your worth is in your very existence.
the most beautiful thing
about you
IS YOU.

don't forget.

affirmations to say out loud

i am a miracle on the road,
a testimony to the beauty of the human soul.
my light shines brightly,
guiding me through the darkness.
i am a work in progress,
a piece of art
transforming with each new experience.
i accept my imperfections.
they make me who I am.
my feelings, my experiences,
and my existence all matter.
the hero I've been waiting for all along
is my inner power.
i am ready to act.
my heart is open, grateful
and able to love deeply,
to forgive with ease,
is the source of my inspiration.
my pain is gone,
i can breathe with joy.
i am never alone.
God, the Universe supports me,
protects me,
loves me,
picks me up when i fall.
i am safe.
i am beautiful, strong and radiant.
i trust and believe in myself.
i release all my fears,
my disbelief and my insecurities.
i let go of judgments and anxious thoughts.
i feel calm and know that everything is okay.
i choose to laugh, to dream,
to believe that everything is possible.
i have the power to create change in my life.

repeat and repeat,
and then repeat it again

Do you have any difficulty thinking or saying positive things about yourself? If so, why?

WHAT WON'T LET ME BE WHO I WANT TO BE?

THE LIMITATION IS IN OUR BELIEFS

Often, what holds us back are our own beliefs. We all have them; it's just part of being human. Beliefs shape the way we see ourselves and the world, influencing our choices and guiding our actions. We acquire them along the way - through experiences, interactions with others, our family, culture, the environment in which we grew up and live, religion, and societal expectations. Over time, they become ingrained in our subconscious mind as an "undeniable truth" about ourselves, when in reality, they have little to do with the truth, because, for various reasons, we have never questioned them. Many of them are outright lies.

These sneaky beliefs can hold us back, trapping us in fear, doubt, and low self-esteem. They can cause pain and prevent growth and healing. Well, the good news is that we have this wonderful and divine gift of awareness. We have the power to observe and reflect, which allows us to distinguish between what serves us and what keeps us stuck in patterns that limit our potential. Recognizing these beliefs and questioning their validity is the first step to changing them and removing the barriers they've built.

You begin to fly
when you let go of self-limiting beliefs and allow your mind and aspirations to rise to greater heights.

- Brian Tracy

they sit in the mind,
quieter than thoughts.
they speak of things
that don't even exist,
walls you cannot cross.
they cloud your dreams,
convinced they know
how you should live.
and though their voice
sounds familiar,
they are nothing more
than an illusion,
a mirage that separates you
from who you want to be.

MY SELF-LIMITING BELIEFS:

Identify and write down negative beliefs you hold about yourself.

Trace the origin and source of your negative beliefs. WHERE DO THEY COME FROM? ARE THEY MY BELIEFS, OR HAVE THEY SOMEHOW BEEN PASSED ON TO ME?

there is so much more in you
than what these beliefs
allow you to see.

start questioning them.
question their truth.
question their weight.
start to unravel them,
thread by thread,

and choose:
what should stay?
what should go?

Think about and write down as much evidence as you can to show
that these statements are not true about who you are.

Limiting Belief	Evidence for Change	New, Empowering Belief

notice your thoughts-
they're the seeds of your future.

nurture the ones
which guide your mind
toward beliefs
that support you to grow.

what other beliefs about myself would I like
to nurture or strengthen?

THE REASONS WHY I AM VALUABLE JUST AS I AM ARE...

NO DISCUSSION.

Kintsugi is the Japanese art of repairing broken pottery with gold. Instead of hiding the cracks, it highlights them – turning what was once broken into something even more beautiful. The same is true for you. Your cracks, your wounds, your scars – they don't diminish your worth. They tell the story of your strength, of what you've survived. The pain you've carried can become part of something new. You don't have to pretend nothing happened. You can gently put yourself back together, piece by piece. And though you may never be exactly the same, you can become whole again – beautiful, real, with golden lines running through the places that once hurt the most.

the wound is the place where the light enters you,

-Rumi

speaking **your truth** might hurt,
but not speaking it
will hurt more

This part may be tough for you and could make you cry. It will take courage to face memories or experiences that feel uncomfortable or have been impacting your life in unhealthy ways.

On the following pages, take some time to write clearly about a traumatic, emotional, or specific experience or problem you are currently struggling with- something deeply personal and important to you. By this, I mean an issue you would like to work through, or an internal wound that you wish to heal. If you feel that something is too difficult or too painful to write about, choose a topic that you frequently think about or worry over. It could be some kind of behavior that's affecting your well-being or a relationship that needs your attention.
Write down all your emotions, feelings, and thoughts about it- honestly and openly. Be authentic. Don't worry about the form or structure, just keep writing without stopping to edit. As you write, consider how this experience might connect to your childhood, relationships, or the people involved. Reflect on how it has affected your past, present, or might affect your future.
Then turn your focus on yourself: who were you before this experience? Who are you now? Who do you want to become?

The idea is to openly acknowledge, accept, and express your blocked feelings so that they can be fully experienced, understood, and healed. It is through processing these experiences that we can free ourselves from the burdens we carry.

WHAT IS MY WOUND?

you can't heal from something
if you deny its existence...

You are doing a great job.
I bow to your strength.

look at it,
name it,
feel it,
say how it hurts you,
cry,
scream if you need to,
let it out of your body,
breathe deeply.

let go of what you can...

This practice is not about reopening old wounds, it's about giving yourself permission to process what's there at your own pace. When you feel ready, you can return to this exercise by choosing the same or another experience that seems significant to you.

Each time it may feel a little lighter, a little clearer. You may uncover new layers of understanding and healing, gradually transforming the pain into wisdom.

life shows us that it will not be easy. pain and suffering are inevitable. it's not my fault. it's not your fault, that's how it is. you are not responsible for your trauma and what happened to you. but you are responsible for how you react to it. you have a choice of what to do with it. you can stay down, in the victim space, or stand up for yourself and the rest of your life.

your trauma or loss doesn't mean you can't still live fully. life is both beautiful and painful – and you can choose to embrace it as a whole, just as it is.

Take a moment to reflect on what emotions came up for you as you wrote about your experience? Did any feelings or thoughts surprise you? How did your body react? It's important to allow yourself to be with whatever comes up without rushing to change it.

Let it all hang out.

today i stroke your cheek, and say:

the past is the past.
you can't change it.
even if you are knocked down,
and have no energy
for this moment,
take a step forward
to a place of hope
and faith in a better tomorrow.
all good things are waiting for you.

don't give up.
you can do it. i know you can.

Sometimes, even the most difficult experiences can offer us something valuable if we're open to learning from them.

WHAT LESSON OR GIFT CAME WITH MY TRAUMA?

pain is a teacher
who doesn't give a damn
about being fair.
but shows you things
you didn't know
about yourself.

WHERE AM I GOING

FROM?   TO?

Difficult roads often lead to beautiful destinations.

what have I been holding on to for too long?

You can't start the next chapter of your life if you're still
reading the last one....

Darkness cannot drive out darkness;
only light can do that.
Hate cannot drive out hate;
*only **love** can do that.*

-Martin Luther King, Jr.

Going back a few years, forgiveness seemed to me a foreign concept, something I could not grasp, let alone practice. Back then, I believed that forgiveness was a lofty act, reserved only for saints. But today I see it differently. Today I know that forgiveness is possible, and is one of the greatest gifts we can give ourselves. Forgiveness is first and foremost about you. It's about freeing your heart from the pain, anger, bitterness and resentment that keep you trapped in the past. Forgiveness allows you to breathe again, regain joy, find inner peace and open yourself to a new beginning, unburdened by yesterday's wounds.

Of course, forgiveness can be extremely difficult. Some wounds are deeper than others, sometimes the thought of letting go seems impossible. Sometimes you have to forgive something to yourself.

So if, despite everything, some part of you still feels resistance, know that I understand. You can't force yourself to forgive. It's a journey that unfolds when your heart is ready for it.

what if nothing in life is random?
what if every moment,
every person,
every challenge
is here to guide you?

what if
everything is part of a bigger picture?

DO I VALUE FORGIVENESS? WHAT IS IT TO ME?

To forgive is to set a prisoner free and discover that the prisoner was you.

-Lewis B. Smedes

IS THERE SOMEONE IN MY LIFE THAT I NEED TO FORGIVE?

WHAT EMOTIONS ARISE WHEN I THINK OF THIS PERSON?

every grudge is poison,
your chosen undoing of peace.
they may have walked away.
but you still pay the price.
let it go.
not for them.
but to feel freedom
weightless and yours again.

what do I hope to accomplish by not forgiving this person?

IF I SAW THIS PERSON AS SOMEONE
who is hurting and in need of healing,
would I feel more open to forgiveness?

what small steps can I take today to start the journey
of forgiveness

WHAT DO I NEED TO FORGIVE MYSELF FOR?

forgive yourself,
because you are human.
because you didn't know better.
mistakes don't define you.
growth does.

I want you to know

- Forgiveness is not an instant shift, nor should it be. It's a process, and it's okay to take small steps toward releasing guilt, shame, and regret.

- Being human means making mistakes. You are not alone in your imperfections; everyone stumbles at some point. It's a natural part of life.

- It's okay to mess up. Mistakes are not a sign of failure; they are opportunities to learn. You are allowed to make mistakes, and forgiving yourself is how you turn those moments into growth.

- You are not defined by your past actions. Every day is a new opportunity to choose differently. The mistakes you've made are part of your journey, not your identity.

- Being kind to yourself is essential. You wouldn't judge or punish a friend the way you've judged yourself. Treat yourself with the same compassion and patience you would extend to someone you love.

- Letting go of past hurts frees your heart. Holding onto regret only weighs you down. Forgiveness is not excusing what happened, but rather releasing its hold on your peace and future.

- Forgiveness does not mean forgetting. You don't need to erase the memory or the lesson from your life. What it means is choosing not to let the past control your present or future.

- Every day is an opportunity to heal. There's no deadline for forgiveness. It's okay to have setbacks or days when it feels harder. Each new moment brings a fresh chance to choose compassion and understanding.

what am I proud of in my journey so far?

WHAT IS MY OVERARCHING INTENTION FOR THIS PHASE OF MY LIFE?

What is the first step I can take toward my intention?

Sometimes, the most powerful thing we can do in our healing is to remember that we always have a choice. Even if the past was hard. Even when habits become automatic. Even when fear speaks loudly. We have the power to choose. Even if it's just one small step, the direction you take is yours to decide.

You don't need to see the whole path ahead. You don't need to be fully prepared for everything. All that matters is that you start with what you feel today, with what you know now. That's enough.

Your life can still be a beautiful story - you choose a narrative to write. Even if your hands are shaking, you can choose to do it with kindness, awareness, and courage.

WHAT DOES IT MEAN TO ME WHEN I SAY,
"I have a choice, I can choose differently "?

TODAY I CHOOSE...

\#

\#

\#

\#

\#

\#

\#

\#

\#

WHAT TRULY MATTERS TO ME RIGHT NOW?
what is trying to break free and come to life within me?

What is it that's calling you to life right now? It could be the passion for a hobby you once loved but haven't made time for. Perhaps it's the desire to connect deeply with others or to feel truly understood. It might be a longing for adventure, the urge to explore new places, or simply to experience joy and playfulness again. These feelings can be subtle but powerful, nudging us toward what we need, reminding us that life has a lot to offer and that we deserve to live it to the full.

what does the word 'life purpose' mean to me?

_____

_____

_____

_____

_____

_____

_____

_____

_____

DO I KNOW WHAT MY PURPOSE IS? IF I AM STILL DISCOVERING IT,
what could it be?

you don't need a grand plan.
you don't need the answers yet.
just be someone
who matters to you.
not the world,
not some far-off dream
-**just you.**
be your life purpose.

start here:
with your own heartbeat.
your own breath,
your own worth.

when you choose yourself,
the rest will come.
the path will appear.

IN MOMENTS OF DOUBT, I WANT TO REMEMBER THAT...

I am strong enough to move through this, even when the path feels difficult. Each step, no matter how small, is progress. I have the right to feel good, to heal, and to live my life fully. Even when everything feels heavy, I know I have the strength to rise up and keep moving forward.

WHAT ARE THE MOMENTS THAT TAKE MY BREATH AWAY
and make me feel fulfilled?

what are the things that make me say:
I love doing this?

Great success begins with small things we do with love.

what are my current goals
List everything you want to do, whenever.

In 5 words, what do I need to achieve these goals?

Imagine that there are no limits, barriers, or obstacles in your way, only endless possibilities. What does your ideal life look like if everything you thought was impossible suddenly became possible? Visualize every detail-what do you see and feel? No dream is too small or too big; every idea is valid.

Choose any form of expression that resonates with you-writing, drawing, painting, or even creating a vision board. Use colors, words, and shapes that speak to your heart. Allow your inner artist to come to life. This is your personal creation, a snapshot of the life you're inviting into existence.

IF I COULD PICTURE MY BEST LIFE, WHAT WOULD IT BE?

WHICH AREAS OF MY LIFE MOST NEED ATTENTION OR NURTURING
right now?

What core values or feelings do I want to prioritize
(e.g., peace, connection, confidence)?

WHAT SITUATIONS IN MY LIFE DO I NEED TO TAKE RESPONSIBILITY FOR?

it's time.
time to stop pointing fingers,
time to stop blaming,
and start owning.

take that step,
make that choice–
to grow,
to become,
to rise again.

no one else can do this for you.

Who supports and strengthens me?

What relationships are most important in my life right now?

HOW DO PEOPLE IN THESE RELATIONSHIPS MAKE ME FEEL?

WHAT DO I DEEPLY DESIRE IN MY RELATIONSHIPS?

Am I able to be open with others,
or do I tend to hide my feelings and needs?

HOW DO I TEND TO RESPOND WHEN I FEEL REJECTED
or misunderstood?

How can I better communicate my needs and emotions?

How do I react when someone tries to get close to me
what happens inside me emotionally or physically?

When do I feel the need to distance or protect myself
in relationships?

HOW DO MY PAST SHAPE THE WAY I FEEL AND THINK ABOUT
closeness, trust, and openness in my relationships today?

Do I give myself permission to walk away from relationships
that hurt me?

WHAT HOLDS ME BACK FROM LETTING GO OF CONNECTIONS
that no longer serve me?

in the silence between us,
new bonds grow softly.
we are afraid–
and yet we still reach out.
a timid smile
blooms into joy.
we wander through storms,
but together, we find the light.
in the warmth of each other,

we heal,

we rise,

we ignite.

what do I need today in order to rebuild or deepen trust
with others (or with myself)?

HOW DO I WANT TO SHOW UP IN MY RELATIONSHIPS
moving forward?

what others see in you
is their internal projection,
based on their own beliefs,
shaped by their experiences,
and tainted by own insecurities.
they can only see fragments,
pieces of themselves
mirrored in you.
let them see.
let them see what they can see.
you are beyond it.
let their judgments drift.

you don't have to prove
anything to anyone.

You have already proven it to yourself.

WHAT COULD I DO TO WORRY LESS ABOUT OTHERS' OPINIONS?

the things you might need to know:

the right people will meet you where you are
  – not where you "should" be.

sometimes the most important relationship to repair
is the one you have with yourself.

you are allowed to want connection and protect your heart.
these two things can live together.

not all connections are meant to last forever,
but each one teaches us something about who we are.

you deserve relationships where your tenderness
is not only safe, but sacred.

people's judgments are more about them than they are
about you.

your worth is not defined by anyone's opinion.

boundaries don't push people away, they create
safe spaces for real connection.

criticism and praise are fleeting–they don't change who
you are.

not taking things personally, viewing them with irony,
or a lighthearted perspective brings you peace.

self-love is your anchor; nurture it.

even if your past taught you to fear closeness,
your future can teach you to feel safe again.

true connection begins when we stop performing
and start being real.

trust doesn't need to rush.

embrace your uniqueness–it's your greatest gift.

ARE THERE CONNECTIONS I STILL CARRY IN MY HEART
that feel wounded, or in need of attention?

WHAT DO I WANT THIS CONNECTION TO MEAN GOING FORWARD?

IS THERE ANYONE I SHOULD APOLOGIZE TO?

who might you heal with a simple word, a humble heart,
a sincere apology?

When you forgive, you free your soul.
But when you say I'm sorry, you free two souls.

– Donald L. Hicks

Write a letter to the person you should say sorry or to whom
you owe something and tell them how you feel about it.

WHAT WOULD I LIKE TO SAY TO MY MOTHER?

WHAT WOULD I WANT MY FATHER TO KNOW?

WHAT DID I NEED MOST AS A CHILD BUT DIDN'T RECEIVE?

if you could just
come back to me,
notice me, hear me.
if you could just
hold me tightly,
make me feel safe.
if you could just
take care of me –
not to fix me,
but let me know
i'm worthy to be loved.

come back to me,
take my hand.
and
bring us both home.

what kind of adult did I need when I was little?

can I be that for myself now?

was there space for emotions in my childhood–tears, anger, fear?
how were they responded to in my environment?

WHAT EMOTIONS IS MY INNER CHILD REPRESSING?

IS THERE A PLACE, MEMORY, OR OBJECT THAT HELPS ME FEEL CLOSE
to my younger self? What does it remind me of?"

If I could give my inner child a gift,
what would it be and why?

hi, i want you to know something:

your voice matters.
your truth matters.
your questions, your thoughts, your feelings
- they matter.
i am sorry that you have been silenced.
that should never have happened.
but now you can speak.
i am here - grown up, mature,
ready to carry your voice.
now it is powerful, it is strong.
don't be afraid.
i am here to support you,
and i will not silence you again.

WHAT DO I WANT MY INNER CHILD TO KNOW?

IF MY INNER CHILD COULD SEND ME A MESSAGE,
what would they tell me?

WHAT QUALITIES DID I HAVE AS A CHILD THAT I MAY HAVE LOST
or hidden along the way? Can I reconnect with them?

WHAT DID I ENJOY AS A CHILD?
can I get back to those things now?

WHEN WAS THE LAST TIME I ALLOWED MYSELF TO FEEL
childlike wonder?

How can I bring more play, joy, or softness
into my life today?

WHEN DO I FEEL MOST VULNERABLE?

Protect your freedom

Imagine a space where your energy connects with other people's energy. This space is like a gateway through which different energies - emotions, thoughts, intentions, and actions - connect and influence each other.
Your task is to nurture this space because it protects who you truly are and what you want. Take care of it by defining your boundaries so that you don't weaken or even destroy yourself under the influence of others.

Every time you honor your needs and feelings, you are telling the world:

This is who I am, and I matter.

I firmly believe that we are not here to change ourselves to fit the needs or expectations of others; we are here to be exactly who we are, authentically and without limits.

WHAT DO I DO JUST BECAUSE I THINK I 'SHOULD,'
even if deep down I feel it's not mine?

HOW OFTEN DO I SAY 'YES' TO PEOPLE WHEN I WOULD RATHER SAY 'NO'?
Why do I do it?

Do I feel like I often abandon parts of myself in order to please or make others happy?

How do I feel when I need to say no or set a boundary?

How would my life be if I allowed myself to make
more decisions on my own?

WHAT ARE THE THINGS I AM NOT OKAY WITH?
where do I need to set clearer boundaries?

lets change the rules.

no more shrinking to please others, saying yes when my heart says no, no more giving all of myself to those who don't even care, no more pushing boundaries when my body needs rest, no more staying silent when my voice has to be heard, no more letting anyone decide for me, no more fixing things that never worked, no more seeking validation from those who can't see my worth, no more giving up my dreams for others' convenience, no more letting people drain my energy. no more "sorry" for my needs. no more feeling guilty when I put myself first.

Write down 10 affirmations that will remind you that
setting boundaries is the right thing to do.

LIVING IN THE PRESENT MOMENT
is the way to HAPPINESS.

Happiness isn't something to chase. It is here and now, in moments that we often overlook.

I am happy when I look at the sky and see the clouds floating by, not rushing, not fighting time. There's so much beauty in being present. There's so much peace in simply being here, without haste, without pressure. We often spend so much time thinking about the past, wishing things had turned out differently, or worrying about what's to come. However, the past is gone, and the future is never guaranteed. There's no sense in dwelling on what we cannot change or predict. The only thing we can control is the present moment, and that's where real power lies. When I stop chasing what's ahead or regretting what's behind, I choose to live fully and experience life as it comes.

That's really powerful.

Pick up your crayons or markers, sit comfortably, and take a deep, calm breath. Let go of any thoughts of the past or future - allow yourself to be in present moment. Focus on the act of coloring, the movement of your hand and the touch of the pencil on the paper. If your mind begins to wander, gently bring your attention back to the shapes, colors and strokes. Let the act of creating anchor you in the present. There is no rush, no judgment - there is only you, your breath and your creation in front of you.

worry pulls you away.
away from here,
from now.
the past is gone,
the future unknown,
and neither is yours
to control.
but this moment,
this breath,
this space
you're in right now
–belongs to you.

be here.

make it count.

WHEN WAS THE LAST TIME I FELT MY BREATH?

Close your eyes for three minutes and feel your breath.

there is nowhere else you need to be.
just this breath in.
just this breath out.
just you, breathing, aware.

Take a moment to sit quietly with yourself. No distractions, no agenda-just you. Feel the peace of simply existing here, without needing to do anything else. There's no pressure. You don't need to think, just be.

Start by noticing how your body feels. Is there any tension in your shoulders, your back, or your jaw? Don't judge it-just notice it. Feel the weight of your body, grounding you to this moment. What do you feel beneath you, supporting you?

Now, turn your attention to your senses. What can you hear? Soft sounds, distant or close? Let them come and go, without needing to label or analyze. Let the sounds be as they are, part of the space around you.

What do you feel on your skin? The air, the temperature, any sensation of touch? Just notice it, without needing to name it.

Look around you-without judgment. Notice the shapes, colors, and textures of the objects near you. Don't analyze them, just see them as they are, present in this moment.

Can you smell anything? The air, the faint scent of something in the space? Don't attach meaning to it, just acknowledge it.

Breathe. Feel the flow of air entering and leaving your body. Let it be natural, without force. Allow yourself to simply exist in this space, without needing anything more. Feel the fullness of being here-without judgment, just presence.

-Congratulations, you've just taken a moment to be fully present.

don't overthink, don't complicate, take a breath

What if there was no need to change anything? What if you simply stopped and felt yourself here, in this moment? Then you would allow yourself just to be–nothing more. No need to judge, no need to fix or improve anything. Just being, here and now, effortlessly accepting what is. Pausing between all the "whens" and "tomorrows" to fully experience the present.

Be here, in this instant, where nothing needs to be complicated. You don't need to rush. You don't need to earn your place. You don't need to prove anything. You don't need to chase after something you can't even name. You don't need to achieve to be worthy.

Nothing exists but this moment. And in it, you can simply be–without pressure, without expectations, without thoughts of the past or the future.

The present moment asks for nothing but your presence. Maybe you hear the wind rustling outside, catch the scent of morning coffee, or feel the warmth of the sun on your skin. Maybe you notice the weight of your feet pressing against the earth, grounding you in the certainty that this is where you belong. Inhale. Exhale. Your heart beats. You are alive. And in this moment, you are enough. There is nothing more you need. Life is whole, and you allow yourself to feel it.

Isn't that a relief? In this one breath, everything is exactly as it should be. Here and now, in this quiet space, happiness is born.

Now is the only time we have, and the only time
we have any control over.

-Richard Carlson

WHAT ACTIVITIES OR PRACTICES HELP ME FEEL MORE GROUNDED
and connected to myself?

WHAT CAN I SAY GOODBYE TO, AND WHAT CAN I SAY HELLO TO
to be more present?

I've learned that gratitude is a special kind of magic–one that has the power to transform things. What feels heavy becomes a little lighter. Darkness softens and becomes more bearable. I've learned that gratitude doesn't just appear on its own; it's something we choose for ourselves. And while it's not always easy, it's a choice that holds the power to change everything. I've learned that gratitude isn't just about big things and perfect moments, but also the small, ordinary ones. Like a sip of water that quenches your thirst, a stranger's smile, or the warmth of a blanket after a long day. I've learned that gratitude helps us notice all the little things we often overlook, even though they've always been there. I've learned that you don't need this, that, and so much more to feel better. Gratitude teaches us to value what we already have, instead of constantly yearning for more. I've learned that gratitude builds relationships, strengthens bonds, and connects people, bringing us closer to one another. I've learned that gratitude can ease pain, lighten its weight, and create space for healing. I've learned that when I choose gratitude, it grows and expands, bringing even more beauty into my life. I have learned that the more thankful I am for the good around me, the more blessings seem to find their way to me. I have learned that gratitude shifts my focus - from what's missing to what's already here, filling my days with a sweet sense of abundance.

I've learned that gratitude isn't just about saying "thank you"– it's a way of living, a conscious choice that makes life more beautiful.

THERE IS ALWAYS, ALWAYS, ALWAYS SOMETHING
to be thankful for.

WHAT AM I GRATEFUL FOR?

there is always something to be grateful for.

that message that made you smile.
that sweet moment of quiet, right after the noise.
that birdsong in the urban hum.
that friend who knows how to listen and not ask.
that tree offering cool shade on a hot day.
that starry night that invites you to dream.
that smell of rain on dry ground.
that first sip of coffee in the morning.
that laughter that lingers after a shared joke.
that feeling of clean sheets when you climb into bed.
that neighbor who always waves hello.

don't wait for the big moments.
gratitude is in the everyday.

WHO ARE THE PEOPLE IN MY LIFE THAT I AM GRATEFUL FOR?

what do I appreciate most about them?

WHAT ARE TEN SMALL THINGS IN MY DAY THAT I OFTEN OVERLOOK
but am grateful for?

WHAT IS A SIMPLE PLEASURE I OFTEN TAKE FOR GRANTED
but am grateful for now?

You don't need to have everything to appreciate what you have.

WHAT CHALLENGE HAVE I FACED
that turned out to be a blessing?

as you tune
into *gratitude*,
you will see
flowers in bloom
where once
were only weeds.

WHAT IS SOMETHING ABOUT MY SURROUNDINGS
(home, nature, etc.) that I cherish?

WHEN DID I MAKE SOMEONE SMILE OR BE HAPPY?
How did I feel at that moment?

WHAT ACT OF KINDNESS THAT I HAVE EXPERIENCED
or witnessed has touched my heart?

Write yourself a thank-you note. Thank yourself for being here, for showing up, even if it's not always easy. You have done more than you know. Take a moment to appreciate the effort, resilience, and faith you have given yourself along the way. You deserve this moment of gratitude as well.

thank you for
being so strong
and showing up every day,
even when it was hard.
i see the effort
you have put into it.
you kept going,
even when doubt
tried to take over.
thank you for
being patient and resilient,
even when you
didn't feel like it.
thank you for
the courage you show
with each new beginning.

[from me to myself]

Write a gratitude letter to God, a higher power, or the universe for all the blessings, things, experiences, and people you have met along your path.

Beautiful soul,

Thank you from the bottom of my heart for choosing this journal and walking this path. If these pages have helped you take even a small step closer to the goal or intention you set at the start, then my work has been worthwhile and truly meaningful to me.

I would be deeply grateful if you could share your thoughts by leaving a review. Your voice matters—not just to me, but to others who might find inspiration and value in these pages.

We are all part of the same journey—a vast tapestry where every thread has its unique place and purpose. I believe we are deeply connected, and our lives find meaning through our shared pursuit of goodness, love, and mutual support.

Thank you for allowing our paths to cross, even briefly. May your journey ahead be filled with light, beauty, and harmony with your truest self.

With gratitude and faith in unity:

Anna

Made in the USA
Columbia, SC
17 June 2025